Word Detectives Worksheets

Student Pages for Learning Latin Roots through Stories, Movements, and Pictures to Expand Vocabulary

Written and Illustrated by Trista Gleason
in Collaboration with LuAnn Scott, M.S. CCC-SLP

Volume 1

Word Detectives Worksheets

Student Pages for Learning Latin Roots through
Stories, Movements, and Pictures
to Expand Vocabulary

This book belongs to:

_____

This workbook is intended to accompany *Word Detectives Volume 1*. *Word Detectives Worksheets Volume 1* will keep student work organized and eliminate the need for copies.

Stories and movements are not included in these pages. The entirety of this workbook in addition to the stories, the movements, and the instructor's guide can be found *Word Detective Volume 1*. This workbook contains a picture for each root which students can color, the worksheets for each of the four lessons, and prefix and suffix indexes.

Acknowledgements

<u>Unlocking Literacy, Effective Decoding & Spelling Instruction</u> by Marcia K. Henry

The selection and order of Latin Roots are based on Henry's recommendation in her book. For additional activities, and lists of words arranged by prefix, suffix, Latin root, and Greek combining form, please consult this extraordinary book.

Dictionary.com

This outstanding website not only provided me with numerous definitions, but it also listed word origin and history. This website was invaluable to me and is an excellent free resource for students.

Eisenhower Elementary School, Fort Leavenworth, KS

Principals Marlene Black and Cindy Wepking, the second grade team, Melissa Heinen, Cymbre Herringer, Laura Hurd, and Stacy Lee, my son's first grade teacher Susan Todd, and the rest of the fabulous faculty and staff are responsible for encouraging me to publish this series. They taught my children, and they taught me. Thank you.

LuAnn Scott and Joel P. Gleason

My mother, LuAnn, read to me. She taught me how to read and to love it when I was a little girl. My mother also shared her passion for teaching. Her love of her profession is contagious.

Following a very full day at the office, my husband, Joel, spent his nights helping me come up with silly stories, taking vocabulary tests, and editing and revising this workbook. To you both: thank you, and I love you.

Mary M. Bethune Elementary, Hollywood, Florida

Principal Mary Lou Ridge, and teachers Cheryll Best, Katherine Bennett, Marta Moise, Dawn Fein and Louise Carpenter allowed LuAnn to step out of the box and develop new methods by combining parts of many different programs with the best elements of their teaching. They provided valuable feedback concerning what works and what does not work within classrooms. Thank you.

Table of Contents

Attention Students:

★ ★ ★ ★ ★ ★ ★ ★ ★ ★

Word Detective Vacancy

Now seeking dedicated students for intense training in word detection.

Applicants must know the secret code (how letters turn sounds into words).

- Applicants should be able to read large, unfamiliar words.
- Applicants should be able to associate sounds with specific letters in the word.
- Applicants should be able to dissect large words into syllables.

★ ★ ★ ★ ★ ★ ★ ★ ★ ★

Morphemes

- *Morphemes are the basic meaningful parts of words.*

- *Prefixes are usually at the beginning, roots in the middle, and suffixes at the end.*

- *Morphemes are clues to the meaning of a word.*

- *Morphemes explain spelling rule-breakers and help us to remember how to spell difficult words.*

- *12 Latin roots + 2 Greek combining forms = 100,000 words.[*]*

Your mission, should you choose to accept it, is to learn to search for clues in a word. **Morphemes** are parts of a word that have meaning. You have used them before if you have said, "unzip, uncap, unbuckle, stopped, seated, nodded, or bobbed." Prefixes like "un-" attach to the front of a word, and suffixes like "-ed" attach to the back. Both prefixes and suffixes change what the word means.

We are going to learn about a third kind of morpheme: root morphemes, specifically **Latin roots**. The root is the meaningful part. The rest of the word is built around it. The English language, along with Spanish, French, Italian, and others, developed from the Latin language. Latin roots are hiding in over half of our English words.

Your training will involve memorizing Latin roots and their meaning, and then detecting them inside of English words. If you know what the root means, you may be able to uncover what the word means.

Word Detective training begins with the pretest on the next page.

Training Tools

Story A short, simple story helps you to remember things. It is especially helpful if it is surprising, funny, or if you can relate to the characters. We will use stories to help you remember the meaning of the Latin roots.

Movement Feeling with your body is an important part of helping you remember. The body movements will help you associate the root with a meaning and remind you of the story. Let your muscles be your memory.

Picture Simple drawings will help you remember the story, the movement, and the meaning of the roots. You can even make a copy of the drawings and hang them up where you will see them.

[*] Brown, 1947

Latin Roots Pretest (Vol. 1)

Circle the correct meaning for each **bold** word. <u>The correct meaning is one of the options</u>, but if one doesn't stand out to you more than the other two, circle D) "I don't know". You are not expected to know what most of these words mean. How many correct meanings can you circle?

1. transform
A) change shape
B) robot part
C) move
D) "I don't know"

2. export
A) criminal
B) carry away
C) excite
D) "I don't know"

3. corrupt
A) broken morals
B) mechanical
C) suddenly
D) "I don't know"

4. distract
A) stop running
B) reject an invitation
C) draw attention away
D) "I don't know"

5. transcribe
A) to complain
B) signal with a radio
C) make a written copy
D) "I don't know"

6. spectacle
A) obeying laws
B) a public sight
C) fishing gear
D) "I don't know"

7. structure
A) a building
B) impressive action
C) a German pastry
D) "I don't know"

8. inflection
A) difficulty moving
B) curve in voice pitch
C) splattered paint
D) "I don't know"

9. dictate
A) tell one what to do
B) dislike a food
C) unpleasant
D) "I don't know"

10. conifer
A) discuss together
B) bearing pinecones
C) undesirable acquaintance
D) "I don't know"

11. emit
A) undo an error
B) frog anatomy
C) send forth
D) "I don't know"

12. aqueduct
A) flightless bird
B) blue-green coloring
C) device to lead water
D) "I don't know"

13. credible
A) easily made
B) worthy of belief
C) able to be eaten
D) "I don't know"

14. divert
A) turn from a path
B) journey underwater
C) intersect
D) "I don't know"

15. propulsion
A) agreement
B) pushing forward
C) pulling back
D) "I don't know"

16. facile
A) easily done
B) eyes, nose, or lips
C) waste products
D) "I don't know"

You don't need to go over your answers now. Save them to compare to your Post-test. See how much you learn in your Word Detective Training!

Lesson 1

form, port, rupt, tract

form

to shape

port

to carry

rupt

to burst

tract

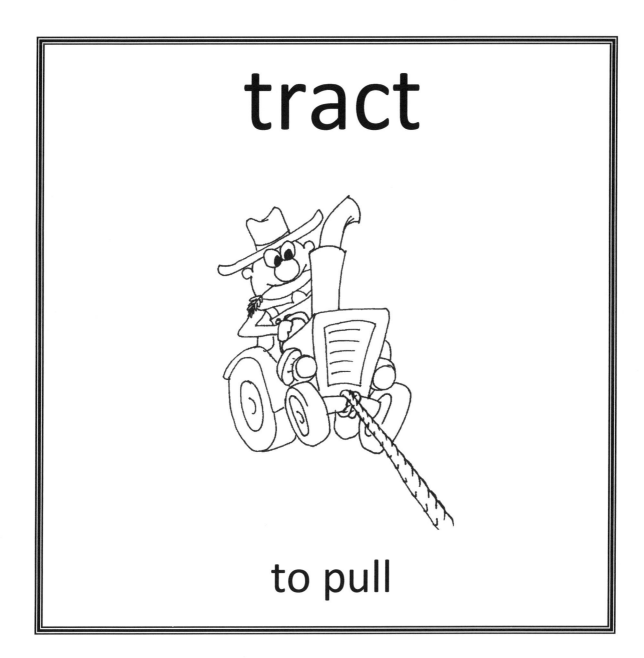

to pull

Use the Roots, Lesson 1

form to shape

Underline the Latin root in each word in the box.

deformed	formal	conform	formulated	transformer
information	form	informant	uniform	misinformed

Use clues that the prefixes or suffixes give you, or use a dictionary to match each word to a definition below. Write the word next to the definition.

_____*inform*_____ shape the mind or teach

_____ one who shapes your mind (teaches or provides new material) about someone else

_____ knowledge, material that shapes the mind

_____ shaped the mind in the wrong way, given bad information

_____ change shape in order to go with something

_____ one shape, identical (can be identical clothing)

_____ something that changes the shape (of itself or something else)

_____ put out of shape, disfigured

_____ shaped a method or procedure, thought of

_____ describes something that is the agreed upon shape, method, or ceremony

_____ shape

port 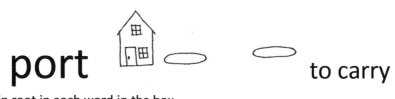 to carry

Underline the Latin root in each word in the box.

teleport	airport	transport
transported	unimportant	portal

Use clues that the prefixes or suffixes give you, or use a dictionary to match each word to a definition below. Write the word next to the definition.

_____ door or gate, an entrance which carries to another place

_____ carried across

_____ point from which and to which things are carried by air

_____ carry over a distance instantaneously

_____not carrying much weight or consequence

_____carry across

rupt to break or burst

Underline the Latin root in each word in the box.

erupted	abrupt	interrupted	disruption

Use clues that the prefixes or suffixes give you, or use a dictionary to match each word to a definition below. Write the word next to the definition.

_____ sudden change, unexpected, breaking the routine

_____ something that breaks something apart or causes disorder

_____ broke into the middle of something

_____ burst out

tract  to draw or pull

Underline the Latin root in each word in the box.

detract	distractible	attracted	protracted	tractor

Use clues that the prefixes or suffixes give you, or use a dictionary to match each word to a definition below. Write the word next to the definition.

_____ pulled toward

_____ able to be pulled away

_____ a vehicle used for pulling farm machinery

_____ to draw (pull) away, take away

_____ drawn out or lengthened (think of pulling the ending farther and farther forward), made longer

Do the movement for each picture. Write the root and the meaning inside the box by the picture.

13

Underline the root in the bold word. Use what you know about the meaning of the root to select the best definition.

1) **detract**

A) to prefer using a treadmill
B) to record a part of music
C) to draw away or divert
D) I don't know

2) **formation**

A) troops standing in columns or squares
B) something that makes documents
C) yes votes
D) I don't know

3) **abrupt**

A) stomach definition
B) changing suddenly, unexpected
C) continued strength
D) I don't know

4) **portfolio**

A) recommended wine pairing
B) boat part
C) a flat case for carrying papers
D) I don't know

Lesson 2
scrib, spec, stru, flect

scrib, script

to write

spec, spect, spic

to see or sort

stru, struct, stry

to build

flect, flex

to bend

Use the Roots, Lesson 2

scrib, script 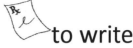 to write

Underline the Latin root in each word in the box.

| subscribe | manuscript | prescription | prescribes | scribbled |

Use clues that the prefixes or suffixes give you, or use a dictionary to match each word to a definition below. Write the word next to the definition.

_____ an order written by a doctor before being given to a pharmacist, medication order

_____ written by hand, a handwritten book or document, or handwriting

_____ was able to write carelessly or meaninglessly

_____ to write underneath, to pledge, to agree

_____ writes beforehand, gives written directions

spec, spect, spic to see, sort

Underline the Latin root in each word in the box.

| perspective | despicable | inspector | retrospect | conspicuous | species |

Use clues that the prefixes or suffixes give you, or use a dictionary to match each word to a definition below. Write the word next to the definition.

_____ easily seen or noticed, attracting special attention

_____ able to be looked down on, despised

_____ a kind or type

_____ to look back in thought, contemplate the past

_____ causing to look at through a point of view

_____ one who looks into carefully, examines

We are going to look at words that contain one of two Latin roots. Each of these roots has multiple forms. You may find it helpful to say all of the forms, do the movement, and say the meaning after you underline the root.

stru, struct, stry to build

flect, flex  to bend

Underline the Latin root in each word in the box.

destruction	inflection	inflexible	instrumental	industry
genuflection	construction	reflect	construe	deflect

Use clues that the prefixes or suffixes give you, or use a dictionary to match each word to a definition below. Write the word next to the definition.

_____ change in pitch or tone of the voice, bend in the voice

_____ the act of pulling down, burning, making useless

_____ to build within, activity, systematic work, productive enterprises in a particular field

_____ to be turned or cast back, as light

_____ important, necessary, like a tool to build toward a goal

_____ an act of bending the knee in reverence

_____ to bend down, turn aside, turn from a true course

_____ the act of building by putting together parts

_____ to give meaning to, to pile up together

_____ not able to be bent

22

Do the movement for each picture. Write the root and the meaning in the box by the picture.

The words below contain one of the eight Latin roots you have learned.

flect, flex   form   port   rupt

scrib, script   spec, spect, spic   stru, struct, stry   tract

Underline the root in the bold word. Use what you know about the meaning of the root to select the best definition.

1) circumflex

A) winding around, a vowel under a bent mark
B) a trucker adjective describing mud flaps
C) difficult academic topics, theoretical
D) I don't know

2) uniformity

A) different point of view, disagreement
B) obedient, following orders
C) overall same shape, homogeneity, or regularity
D) I don't know

3) restructure

A) to confine or keep within limits
B) to change the mode of building or parts
C) rest, take a break from activities
D) I don't know

4) support

A) diversion, recreation, pleasant pastime
B) to bear, hold up, carry the weight
C) a meal in the evening
D) I don't know

5) traction

A) an act that one consciously wills
B) parallel lines with rails
C) the act of pulling, a sticking force
D) I don't know

6) suspicion

A) an earnest desire for achievement
B) a doubt, a reason to look at carefully
C) stoppage of payments or debts
D) I don't know

7) corruptible

A) able to be destroyed, morally breakable
B) unable to be changed
C) capable of being restored
D) I don't know

8) inscribe

A) capacity for learning
B) not having the necessary ability
C) to write in or on
D) I don't know

9) special

A) different from what is ordinary, particular kind
B) a small spot or mark as on skin
C) running around a fixed point or center
D) I don't know

10) performance

A) a previous decision
B) a prior right or claim as to payment, choice
C) a thing that provides shape to an idea or character
D) I don't know

Lesson 3
dic, fer, mit, duc

dic, dict

to say

fer

to bear or yield

mit, miss

to send

duc, duce, duct

to lead

Use the Roots, Lesson 3

.dic, dict to say

Underline the Latin root in each word in the box.

contradict	predict	verdict	abdicate	edict

Use clues that the prefixes or suffixes give you, or use a dictionary to match each word to a definition below. Write the word next to the definition.

_____ to declare or tell in advance; prophesy; foretell

_____ to give up or renounce; proclaim away; say you don't want it

_____ to speak the contrary or opposite of

_____ a decree issued by authority; proclamation sent out to subjects

_____ declare what is true; judgment; decision

fer to bear or yield

Underline the Latin root in each word in the box.

circumference	fertile	referee	transfer	offer	suffer

Use clues that the prefixes or suffixes give you, or use a dictionary to match each word to a definition below. Write the word next to the definition.

_____ one who carries others back to a source of information in order to make a decision or ruling; judge

_____ bearing, producing, or capable of bearing crops or offspring

_____ to bear under; undergo or feel pain or distress

_____ the outer boundary of a circle; the path born around a point

_____ to present for acceptance or rejection; to carry to, to bring

_____ to carry across; move from one place or person to another

We are going to look at words that contain one of two Latin roots. Each of these roots has multiple forms. You may find it helpful to say all of the forms, do the movement, and say the meaning after you underline the root.

mit, miss to send or let go

duc, duce, duct  to lead

Underline the Latin root in each word in the box.

permit	introduce	reduction	commit	educate
emissary	conduct	emit	submit	abduct

Use clues that the prefixes or suffixes give you, or use a dictionary to match each word to a definition below. Write the word next to the definition.

_____ one who is sent out, a representative sent on a mission

_____ the state of being brought back, lowered in rank, lessened

_____ to lead in, bring in; present to another so as to make acquainted

_____ put under; let go of power and send it to another

_____ carry off or lead away, kidnap

_____ to send through, allow

_____ to send out, discharge, release

_____ to lead out of ignorance, make qualified

_____ to send to join together, pledge, promise

_____ to lead or bring together; management of others or self

Do the movement for each picture. Write the root and the meaning in the box by the picture.

The words below contain one of the twelve Latin roots you have learned.

form	port	rupt	tract	scrib, script	spec, spect, spic
stru, struct, stry	flect, flex	dic, dict	fer	mit, miss	duc, duce, duct

Underline the root in the bold word. Use what you know about the meaning of the root to select the best definition.

1) confer

A) a three dimensional pointed shape
B) to perplex or amaze, confuse, bewilder
C) gather together, compare, bring together
D) I don't know

2) inspector

A) one who looks into carefully, examines
B) one who teaches at a college or university
C) one who has three pairs of legs and two wings
D) I don't know

3) ductile

A) of, pertaining to, or affecting the sense of touch
B) capable of being drawn out into wires or threads
C) performing what is expected or required
D) I don't know

4) postscript

A) to put off to a later time, defer
B) additional phrase after the conclusion of a letter
C) a subterranean chamber or vault
D) I don't know

5) indicate

A) be a sign of, show, make known
B) lacking definition, vague or indistinct
C) having good understanding, comprehension
D) I don't know

6) omit

A) having complete or unlimited knowledge
B) a celestial body moving about the sun
C) fail to do, make, use, send; leave out
D) I don't know

7) infrastructure

A) built below a system or organization, framework
B) invisible light, electromagnetic radiation
C) characterized by looking into oneself
D) I don't know

8) abstract

A) utterly hopeless, humiliating, wretched
B) the posterior section of the body
C) withdrawn or separated from material objects
D) I don't know

9) deport

A) a person representing a constituency
B) to send or carry off
C) a spouse of a reigning monarch
D) I don't know

10) intermittent

A) taking place between two or more institutions
B) a time through which something lasts
C) alternately sending and not sending signals
D) I don't know

Lesson 4
cred, vert, pel, fac

cred

to believe

vert, vers

to turn

pel, puls

to push

fac, fact, fect, fic

to make or do

Use the Roots, Lesson 4

cred  to believe

Underline the Latin root in each word in the box.

credit	incredible	accreditation	incredulous	credo

Use clues that the prefixes or suffixes give you, or use a dictionary to match each word to a definition below. Write the word next to the definition.

_____ something that brings belief to; certification; authority

_____ so extraordinary that it is believed to be impossible

_____ "I believe," a formula of beliefs

_____ not believing, skeptical

_____ trust something will be cared for, paid back; acknowledge, honor

vert, vers to turn

Underline the Latin root in each word in the box.

converse	subvert	versatile	vertical	diverse

Use clues that the prefixes or suffixes give you, or use a dictionary to match each word to a definition below. Write the word next to the definition.

_____ to turn a phrase with another, talk

_____ different, turned apart, a wide range

_____ turned up to the highest point overhead, straight up and down

_____ turn from underneath, overthrow, destroy

_____ capable of turning from one task to another, having many uses

We are going to look at words that contain one of two Latin roots. Each of these roots has multiple forms. You may find it helpful to say all of the forms, do the movement, and say the meaning after you underline the root.

pel, puls   to drive or push

fac, fact, fect, fic   to make or do

Underline the Latin root in each word in the box.

dispel	infect	fictional	pulse	facilitate
impulsive	compel	benefactor	repulsion	sufficient

Use clues that the prefixes or suffixes give you, or use a dictionary to match each word to a definition below. Write the word next to the definition.

_____ pushed from within, swayed by emotions, rash

_____ something that is made up, imaginary

_____ to drive in various directions, to push away, disperse

_____ the state of being pushed away, driven back, disgusted

_____ a well to-do person who makes things easier, supporter, patron

_____ throb, beat, to push blood through vessels

_____ to make or do inside of something, taint, spread impurity in

_____ having made up to the needed amount; adequate, enough

_____ to make easier, less difficult; cause to be doable

_____ to drive together (cattle), force (people)

Do the movement for each picture. Write the root and the meaning in the box by the picture.

The words below contain one of the sixteen Latin roots you have learned.

cred	dic, dict	duc, duce, duct	fac, fact, fect, fic	fer	flect, flex
form	mit, miss	pel, puls	port	rupt	scrib, scrip
spec, spect, spic		stru, struct, stry	tract		vert, vers

Underline the root in the bold word. Use what you know about the meaning of the root to select the best definition.

1) expulsion

A) to lay open to danger, attack or harm
B) pertaining to or characterized by an axis
C) the state of being driven out or ejected
D) I don't know

2) dictum

A) something said with authority, a pronouncement
B) disagreeable behavior
C) producer of small plastic cubes
D) I don't know

3) revert

A) return back to a former habit
B) near a natural stream of water
C) caused or derived from machinery
D) I don't know

4) traduce

A) buying, selling, or exchanging commodities
B) walk aimlessly, never reaching a goal
C) lead across as a spectacle, scorn, speak badly of
D) I don't know

5) credulous

A) a sensation of the skin as from horror or fear
B) willing to believe or trust too readily, gullible
C) mysterious in meaning, puzzling, ambiguous
D) I don't know

6) impel

A) act of a mischievous child
B) not strictly belonging, applicable, or correct
C) to drive forward, press on
D) I don't know

7) faction

A) the act of sensing with the eyes
B) a making or doing, a group, a political party, class
C) a positively charged atom or group of atoms
D) I don't know

8) portage

A) carrying boats and goods over land to water
B) a thick food made of meal boiled in milk or water
C) an overwhelming quantity or explosion
D) I don't know

9) inference

A) to make furious, enrage
B) something that comes in opposition, gets in the way
C) a conclusion that has been yielded based on reason
D) I don't know

10) scribacious

A) having a tendency to write too much
B) remarkable, outstanding, bold, brazen
C) like discovering hidden knowledge of the future
D) I don't know

Movement
Review

cred

to believe

dic, dict

to say

duc, duce, duct

to lead

form

to shape

Let's say the root, and do the movements as we say what they mean.

Cred [Point to your super brain as you say…]: to believe.

Dic, dict [starting at your mouth draw a speech bubble with your finger as you say…]: to say.

Duc, duce, duct [motion for someone to follow you]: to lead.

Form [move your hands in front of your face around the round belly as you say…]: to shape.

fac, fact, fect, fic

to make or do

fer

to bear or yield

flect, flex

to bend

mit, miss

to send

Fac, fact, fect, fic [stir the batter]: to make or do.

Fer [lift your palms forward and up]: to bear or yield.

Flect, flex [raise your arm and bend your body forward in a curve as you say…]: to bend.

Mit, miss [toss from out from your stomach]: to send or let go.

pel, puls

to drive or push

port

to carry

rupt

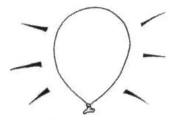

to break or burst

scrib, script

to write

Pel, puls [push your hands together over your heart]: to drive or push.

Port [move your stacked hands up and over as you say...]: to carry.

Rupt [burst your hands apart in front of your face as you say...]: to break or burst.

Scrib, script [pretend to write a cursive e as you say...]: to write.

spec, spect, spic	stru, struct, stry
	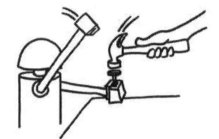
to see, sort	to build
tract	vert, vers

to pull	to turn

Spec, spect, spic [put your hand to your brow and move your head as you slowly scan the room and then point to the ground next to you as you say…]: to see, sort.

Stru, struct, /strEE/ [hammer your right fist onto your left as you say…]: to build.

Tract [pretend you are pulling a rope in front of you as you say…]: to pull.

Vert, vers [spin your finger in a circle]: to turn.

Congratulations!

Take the Post-test on the next page and compare it to your Pretest.

Please continue your training with:

Word Detective Vol. 2

Word Detective Vol. 3

Name _____

Date _____

Latin Roots Post-test (Vol. 1)

Circle the correct meaning for each **bold** word. <u>The correct meaning is one of the options</u>, but if one doesn't stand out to you more than the other two, circle D) "I don't know". How many correct meanings can you circle now?

1. **transform**
A) change shape
B) robot part
C) move
D) "I don't know"

2. **export**
A) criminal
B) carry away
C) excite
D) "I don't know"

3. **corrupt**
A) broken morals
B) mechanical
C) suddenly
D) "I don't know"

4. **distract**
A) stop running
B) reject an invitation
C) draw attention away
D) "I don't know"

5. **transcribe**
A) to complain
B) signal with a radio
C) make a written copy
D) "I don't know"

6. **spectacle**
A) obeying laws
B) a public sight
C) fishing gear
D) "I don't know"

7. **structure**
A) a building
B) impressive action
C) a German pastry
D) "I don't know"

8. **inflection**
A) difficulty moving
B) curve in voice pitch
C) splattered paint
D) "I don't know"

9. **dictate**
A) tell one what to do
B) dislike a food
C) unpleasant
D) "I don't know"

10. **conifer**
A) discuss together
B) bearing pinecones
C) undesirable acquaintance
D) "I don't know"

11. **emit**
A) undo an error
B) frog anatomy
C) send forth
D) "I don't know"

12. **aqueduct**
A) flightless bird
B) blue-green coloring
C) device to lead water
D) "I don't know"

13. **credible**
A) easily made
B) worthy of belief
C) able to be eaten
D) "I don't know"

14. **divert**
A) turn from a path
B) journey underwater
C) intersect
D) "I don't know"

15. **propulsion**
A) agreement
B) pushing forward
C) pulling back
D) "I don't know"

16. **facile**
A) easily done
B) eyes, nose, or lips
C) waste products
D) "I don't know"

Prefix Appendix

The following is based on the prefix appendix in <u>Unlocking Literacy</u> by Marcia K. Henry. Please consult her book for lists of words using each prefix and learning activities. If a prefix is not included in this list, we recommend you consult www.dictionary.com which breaks words into morphemes and lists origin and history.

Prefixes

Prefixes modify a root.
They do not stand alone.
They are used at the beginning of a word.

Three Kinds of Prefixes

- Some prefixes are only spelled one way and only mean one thing. Students may be able to think of familiar words containing these prefixes to determine what they mean. We will call these <u>Simple</u> prefixes.

- Some prefixes mean more than one thing. Students need to consider both meanings. We will call these <u>Dual</u> or <u>Multi</u> prefixes.

- Some prefixes change the way that they are spelled based on the first letter of the word they are modifying. These different spellings are called variants. We will call these <u>Variant</u> prefixes.

    - Variants explain why there are two Rs in "corrupt."
        - Phonetically, the second R is not required.
        - The first R is part of the prefix "cor-" which is a variant of "con-". This variant is used because "rupt" starts with R. We will call "rupt" an R root.
        - The second R is part of the root "rupt."
    - Noting the morphemes may help students to remember the spelling, and reviewing the variants may help students to recognize the meaning of a common prefix spelled in a different way.
    - Variants can often, but not always, be identified by the doubled consonant.
    - Variants are depicted in boxes on the right of the page. These boxes help students to visualize the complexity or simplicity of a prefix.

The variant is determined by the first letter of the root that the prefix is modifying.

Most of the time this box will indicate the first letter of the root, but sometimes the specific root will be listed.

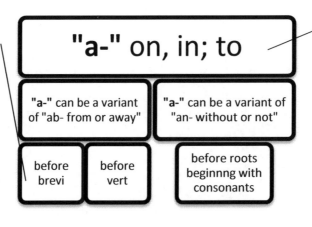

The top box will list the **Base Prefix.** This is the most common meaning of the prefix.

More than one box in the top row indicates multiple meanings.

a- on or in; to (Variant/Multi)
     "A-" usually means "on, in; to."
     Variants of other prefixes are also spelled "a-".
     Students must determine if it is:
          (Simple) "a-" on, in; to
          (Variant) of "ab-" from or away
          (Variant) of "an-" without or not.

ab- from or away (Variant)

ad- to, toward, in, near (Variant)

ambi- both (Simple)

an- without or not (Variant)
     "An-" can be a variant of "ad-" to, toward, in or near before N roots.

     The N will be doubled if the variant of "ad-" meaning "toward" is used.

     It will not be doubled if it means "without or not."

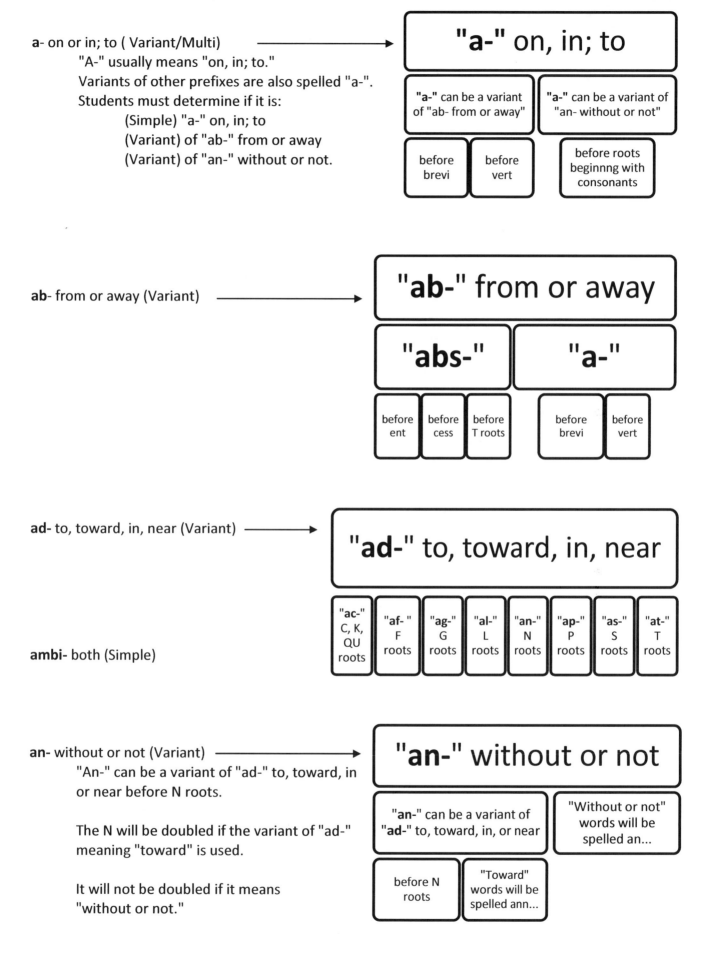

"a-" on, in; to

"a-" can be a variant of "ab- from or away"

"a-" can be a variant of "an- without or not"

before brevi

before vert

before roots beginnng with consonants

"ab-" from or away

"abs-"

"a-"

before ent

before cess

before T roots

before brevi

before vert

"ad-" to, toward, in, near

"ac-" C, K, QU roots

"af-" F roots

"ag-" G roots

"al-" L roots

"an-" N roots

"ap-" P roots

"as-" S roots

"at-" T roots

"an-" without or not

"**an-**" can be a variant of "**ad-**" to, toward, in, or near

"Without or not" words will be spelled an...

before N roots

"Toward" words will be spelled ann...

ante- before (Simple)

anti- opposite or against (Simple)

be- completely, thoroughly, excessively (Simple)

bene- well or good (Simple)

circum- around or about (Simple)

con- together, with, jointly (Variant)

"con-" together, with, jointly

"co-" A or H roots	"col-" L roots	"com-" M, B, P roots	"cor-" R roots

contra- against, opposite, contrasting (Simple)

counter- contrary, opposite (Simple)

de- down or away from (Simple)

dis- not, absence (Variant)

"dis-" not, absence

"dif-" F roots

dys- bad or difficult (Simple)

ex- out or thoroughly (Variant)

"ex-" out or thoroughly

"e-" B, some CL, D, G, J, L, M, R, V roots	"ec-" some C roots	"ef-" F roots

fore- before (Simple)

in- in, on, toward; or not (Dual Variant)

"in-" in, on, toward	"in-" not

"il-" L roots	"im-" B, M, P roots	"ir-" R roots

58

inter- between (Simple)

intra- within (Simple)

intro- in or inward (Simple)

mal- bad, badly; abnormal (Simple)

mid- middle (Simple)

mis- bad, badly, wrong, wrongly (Simple)

multi- many or much (Simple)

non- not or negative (Simple)

ob- (Multi Variant)
  means "extra" (intensifies the root)
  means "down, against facing"
  means "to"

  all 3 variants can use all 3 meanings

"ob-" extra	"ob-" down, against facing	"ob-" to

"oc-" C roots	"of-" F roots	"op-" P roots

per- completely or extra (intensifies the root) (Dual)

post- after, behind, following (Simple)

pre- before (Simple)

pro- forward (Simple)

re- back again; or extra (intensifies the root) (Dual)

se- apart, aside, without (Simple)

sub- under, secondary (Variant)

"sub-" under, secondary

"suc-" C roots	"suf-" F roots	"sug-" G roots	"sup-" some P roots	"sus-" some P or T roots

syn- together, with (Variant)

trans- across, beyond (Simple)

un- (Multi)
  to undo or reverse
  not
  opposite of

"syn-" together, with

"syl-" L roots	"sym-" B, M, or P roots

Numerical Order

1	uni-	**100**	cent-
	mono-	**1,000**	mili-
2	bi-		kilo-
	duo-	**10,000**	myria-
	di-	**Million**	mega-
3	tri-	**Billion**	giga-
	ter-	**Trillion**	tera-
4	quad-, quar-	**Quadrillion**	peta-
	tetra-		
5	quint-		
	pent-		
6	sex-		
	hex-		
7	sept-		
	hept-		
8	octa-, octo-		
9	nona-, nove-		
10	dec-, deca-, deci-		

Alphabetical Order

bi-	2	**octa-**	8
cent-	100	**octo-**	8
dec-	10	**pent-**	5
deca-	10	**peta-**	quadrillion
deci-	10	**quadr-**	4
di-	2	**quar-**	4
duo-	2	**quint-**	5
exa-	quintillion	**sept-**	7
giga-	billion	**sex-**	6
hept-	7	**ter-**	3
hex-	6	**tera-**	4
kilo-	1,000	**tetra-**	4
mega-	million/large	**tri-**	3
mille-	1,000	**uni-**	1
mono-	1		
myria-	10,000		
nona-	9		
nove-	9		

60

Suffix Appendix

The following collection of suffixes is based on the appendix found in <u>Unlocking Literacy</u> by Marcia K. Henry. Please consult her book for lists of words containing each suffix as well as suggested learning activities.

Suffixes

Suffixes modify a word's meaning, often by changing its part of speech.

- The roots are usually derived from verbs.

- Suffixes change roots into nouns, adjectives, adverbs, and sometimes back to verbs.

- Words can contain multiple suffixes.

- Bad Breath E is frequently dropped when adding a suffix.

- Words ending in Y.

  - Words in English do not end with "i". The letter "i" is so skinny, it might fall over at the end of a word, so you have to put a brace on it. This brace turns it into a letter "y." In fact, the only word in English that end with "i" is the word "I," and it has a brace on the top and the bottom that keep it from falling over. Think of the words "my", "boy", "day", and "by."

  - Adding a suffix to words ending in Y

    - If Y has a vowel buddy (oy, ay), then the Y remains, as in "toyed, "swayed".

    - If the suffix being added starts with I, then the Y usually remains to avoid "ii," as in "allying," "crying," "lobbyist."

    - Otherwise, remove the brace, changing Y to I before adding a suffix, as in "allied," "cried," lobbied."

- Naughty Endings are made up of the last letter of a root plus a suffix. See page viii in the front of the book for further details regarding Naughty Endings.

-able: able, can do; **adj** ⟶ "**-able**": able, can do; **adj**

"**-ability**" = "-able" + "-ity"; **noun**

"**-ible**": able, can do; **adj** (Latin roots)

"**-ibility**": **noun** (Latin roots)

-ade: result of action; **noun**

-age: collection, mass, relationship; **noun**

-al, -ial: relating to, characterized by; **adj** ⟶ "**-al**," "**-ial**": relating to, characterized by; **adj**

"**-cial**"

"**-tial**"

base ends C

base ends T

-an: relating to; **adj** or **noun** ⟶ "**-an**": relating to; **adj** or **noun**

"**-ian**": person relating to; **noun**

"**-cian**", "**-tian**", "**-sian**", "**-gian**": all variants using the last letter of the base: person relating to; **noun**

-ant: person of action or state; **noun** or **adj** ⟶ "**-ant**": person of action or state; **noun**

"**-ant**": state; **adj**

"**-ance**": **noun**

"**-ancy**": "-ance" + "-y" **noun**

-ar: **adj**
    (sometimes these letters just the end a noun
    and are not a suffix: sugar, molar, cigar)

-ard: one habitually or excessively in a specified condition; **noun**

-ary: "-ar" + "-y"
>   relating to, place where; **noun**
>   **adj**

-ate:
>   cause or make; **verb**
>   **adj**

-cide: kill; **noun**
>   (same origin as Latin root cise: to cut)

-cy: state, condition, quality; **noun** ⟶

"**-cy**": state, condition, quality; **noun**

"**-acy**": noun

-dom: quality, realm, office, state; **noun**

-ed: past tense; **verb**

-ee: one who receives an action; **noun**

-eer: one associated with; **noun**
>   "-ee" + "-er"

-en: made of; **adj**

-ence: action, state of, quality; **noun**

-ency: action, state, quality; **noun**
>   "-ence" + "-y"

-ent: referent; **noun**
>   **adj**

"**-ent**": referent; **noun**

"**-ent**": adj

"**-ence**": noun

"**-ency**": noun

-er: ⟶
>   one who, that which; **noun** non-Latin roots
>   same meaning as "-or" Latin roots
>   comparative degree, more; **adj**

"**-er**": one who, that which; **noun**

"**-er**": comparative degree, more; **adj**

-ery: relating to, quality, place where; **noun**
>   "-er" + "-y"

-ess: feminine; **noun**

-est: superlative degree, most; **adj**

-ette: small or diminutive; **noun**

-fold: related to a specified amount; **noun**

-ful: full of, full; **adj, noun**

-fy, -ify: make; **verb**

-hood: condition, state, quality; **noun**

-ial, -al: relating to, characterized by; **adj**

-ian: one having a certain skill/art; **noun**

-ic: of, pertaining to, characterized by; **adj**

-ify, -fy: make; **verb**

-ile: relating to, suited for, capable of; **noun**

-ine: nature of; **noun, adj**

-ing: present tense; **verb**

-ion: act of, state of, result of; **noun**

-ish: origin, nature, resembling; **adj**

-ism: doctrine, system, manner, condition, act, characteristic; **noun**

-ist: one who; **noun**

-ite: nature or quality of, mineral product; **noun**

-ium: chemical element or group; **noun**
     "**-ia**" is the plural noun suffix

-ive: causing or making; **adj**

-ize: make; **verb**
     "**-ism**" noun
     "**-ist**" noun

-less: without; **adj**

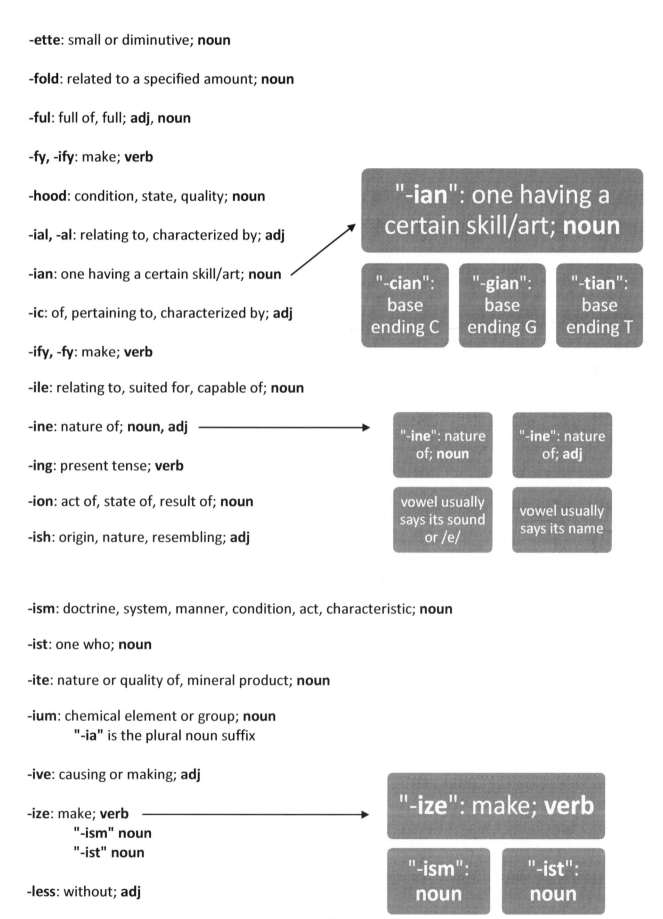

"**-ian**": one having a certain skill/art; **noun**

"**-cian**": base ending C | "**-gian**": base ending G | "**-tian**": base ending T

"**-ine**": nature of; **noun** — vowel usually says its sound or /e/

"**-ine**": nature of; **adj** — vowel usually says its name

"**-ize**": make; **verb**

"**-ism**": noun | "**-ist**": noun

-ling: very small; diminutive; **noun**

-logy: science or study of; **noun** ──────────►

"**-logy**": science or study of; **noun**

"**-ology**"

"**-ologist**" = -ology + -ist: one who deals with/studies a topic; **noun**

-ly: like or manner; **adj**

-ment: act, state, result of an action; **noun**

-most: most or nearest to; **superlative adj**

-ness: state of; **noun**

-or: who, that which; **noun** (Latin roots)

-ory: "-or" + "-y"
     relating to, quality place where; **noun**
     pertaining to, characterized by; **adj**

-ous: full of, having; **adj** ──────────►
     many Naughty Endings formed
     with the base

-ous: full of having; **adj**

-ious, -cious, -gious, -sious, -tious, -xious are all variants using the last letter of the base

-s: plural noun
     "-es" following S, X, CH, SH, Z

-ship: office, state, dignity, skill, quality, profession; **noun**

-some: characterized by a specified quality, condition, or action; **adj**

-ster: one who is associated with, participates in, makes or does; **noun**

-tude: condition, state, quality of; **noun**

-ty, ity: state of or quality of; **noun**

-ure: state of, process, function, office; **noun**
     "-ture," "-sure"

-ward: expressing direction; **adj**

-y: inclined to; **adj**

References

Brown, J. I. 1947. Reading and vocabulary: 14 master words. In M. J. Herzberg (Ed.), Word study, 1-4. Springfield, MA: G & C Merriam.

> *The importance of Latin in the English Language is best summarized by this idea: 12 Latin roots plus 2   Greek combining forms could produce 100,000 English words.*

www.Dictionary.com

> *This free website lists definitions, origin, morphemes, and word history.*

Heath, Chip and Dan. 2007. Made to Stick: *Why Some Ideas Survive and Others Die*. New York, NY: Random House Publishing.

> *The SUCCES concept of using stories to make things stick discussed in this book.*

Henry, M. K. 2010. Unlocking Literacy: *Effective Decoding and Spelling Instruction, 2nd Edition*. Baltimore, Maryland: Paul H. Brookes Publishing Co.

> *This book was the missing link to organizing reading and spelling. The selection of roots and their order as well as the prefix and suffix appendixes are based on this outstanding book. Consult this book for further activities and lists of words sharing common prefixes, suffixes, Latin roots, and Greek combining forms.*

Lindamood, Patricia C. and Phyllis D. 1998. Lindamood Phoneme Sequencing Program for Reading, Spelling, and Speech *The LiPS Program, 3rd Edition*. Austin, Texas: Pro Ed Inc.

> *This outstanding phonics system continues to change lives. It is the key to students learning to decode.*

www.StevensonLearning.com

> *This language system contributed to an understanding of phonics rules, particularly hard and soft C and G.*

www.WilsonLanguage.com

> *This language system also contributed to an understanding of phonics rules.*

Made in the USA
Lexington, KY
06 August 2015